YEAR 5

STAR MATHS STARTERS

A fresh approach to mental maths

TERMS AND CONDITIONS

IMPORTANT - PERMITTED USE AND WARNINGS - READ CAREFULLY BEFORE USING

Minimum specification:
- PC with a CD-ROM drive and 512 Mb RAM (recommended)
- Windows 98SE or above/Mac OSX.1 or above
- Recommended minimum processor speed: 1 GHz
- Facilities for printing

Julie Cogill and Anthony David

Authors
Julie Cogill and Anthony David

Anthony David dedicates this book to his wife Peachey, and sons Oliver and Samuel.

Editors
Niamh O'Carroll and Mary Nathan

Assistant Editor
Margaret Eaton

Illustrator
Theresa Tibbetts (Beehive Illustration)

Series Designer
Joy Monkhouse

Designers
Melissa Leeke and Shelley Best

Text © 2008 Julie Cogill and Anthony David
© 2008 Scholastic Ltd

CD-ROM development in association with Vivid Interactive

Designed using Adobe InDesign and Adobe Illustrator

Published by Scholastic Ltd
Villiers House, Clarendon Avenue,
Leamington Spa, Warwickshire CV32 5PR
www.scholastic.co.uk

Printed by Tien Wah, Singapore
1 2 3 4 5 6 7 8 9   8 9 0 1 2 3 4 5 6 7

ISBN 978-1407-10011-1

ACKNOWLEDGEMENTS
Extracts from the Primary National Strategy's *Primary Framework for Mathematics* (2006)
www.standards.dfes.gov.uk/primaryframework and the Interactive Teaching Programs originally
developed for the National Numeracy Strategy © Crown copyright. Reproduced under the terms of the
Click Use Licence.

Every effort has been made to trace copyright holders for the works reproduced in this book, and the
publishers apologise for any inadvertent omissions.

British Library Cataloguing-in-Publication Data
A catalogue record for this book is available from the British Library.

Introduction..4

The six Rs..7

Whiteboard hints and tips..8

Objectives grid...10

Planning for the six Rs...12

Activities

Targets...13
Number sentence builder...14
Fairground: counting below zero..15
Number line: decimals..16
Twenty cards (ITP): largest and smallest numbers................17
Bricks: ordering decimals..18
Fractions (ITP)...19
Dominoes: fractions and decimals...20
Finding percentages...21
Scaling up and down..22
Maths Boggle: adding two-digit numbers...............................23
Bingo: times tables up to 10 × 10...24
Bingo: division facts up to 100...25
Multiplication square: common multiples...............................26
Function machine..27
Maths Boggle: tenths and hundredths.....................................28
Shopping..29
Polygons (ITP)...30
Find the alien: coordinates..31
Coordinates (ITP)..32
Reflection square...33
Maps and directions...34
Fixing points (ITP): measuring polygons.................................35
Weighing scales...36
Thermometer (ITP)...37
Measuring jug..38
Ruler (ITP)..39
Area (ITP)...40
Clocks: time difference using 24-hour time.............................41
Data handling (ITP)...42

Photocopiable templates

Targets..43
Fairground: counting below zero..44
Bingo...45
Maps and directions...46

Star Maths Starters diary..47

Introduction

In the 1999 *Framework for Teaching Mathematics* the first part of the daily mathematics lesson is described as 'whole-class work to rehearse, sharpen and develop mental and oral skills'. The Framework identified a number of short, focused activities that might form part of this oral and mental work. Teachers responded very positively to these 'starters' and they were often judged by Ofsted to be the strongest part of mathematics lessons.

However, the renewed *Primary Framework for Mathematics* (2006) highlights that the initial focus of 'starters', as rehearsing mental and oral skills, has expanded to become a vehicle for teaching a range of mathematics. 'Too often the "starter" has become an activity extended beyond the recommended five to ten minutes' (*Renewing the Primary Framework for mathematics: Guidance paper,* 2006). The renewed Framework also suggests that 'the focus on oral and mental calculation has been lost and needs to be reinvigorated'.

Star Maths Starters aims to 'freshen up' the oral and mental starter by providing focused activities that help to secure children's knowledge and sharpen their oral and mental skills. It is a new series, designed to provide classes and teachers with a bank of stimulating interactive whiteboard resources for use as starter activities. Each of the 30 starters offers a short, focused activity designed for the first five to ten minutes of the daily mathematics lesson. Equally, the starters can be used as stand-alone oral and mental maths 'games' to get the most from a spare ten minutes in the day.

About the book

Each book includes a bank of teachers' notes linked to the interactive whole-class activities on the CD-ROM. A range of additional support is also provided, including planning grids, classroom resources, generic support for using the interactive whiteboard in mathematics lessons, and an objectives grid.

Objectives grid

A comprehensive two-page planning grid identifies links to the *Primary Framework for Mathematics* strands and objectives. The grid also identifies one of six starter types, appropriate to each interactive activity (see page 7 for further information).

Starter Number	Star Starter Title	Page No.	Strand	Learning objective as taken from the Primary Framework for Mathematics	Type of Starter
16	Maths Boggle: tenths and hundredths	28	Calculating	Use efficient written methods to add and subtract whole numbers and decimals with up to two places	Refine
17	Shopping	29	Calculating	Use efficient written methods to add and subtract whole numbers and decimals with up to two places	Refine
18	Polygons (ITP)	30	Understanding shape	Identify, visualise and describe properties of rectangles, triangles and regular polygons	Refresh
19	Find the alien: coordinates	31	Understanding shape	Read and plot coordinates in the first quadrant	Reason
20	Coordinates (ITP)	32	Understanding shape	Read and plot coordinates in the first quadrant	Refine
21	Reflection square	33	Understanding shape	Complete patterns with up to two lines of symmetry; draw the position of a shape after a reflection	Refine
22	Maps and directions	34	Understanding shape	Estimate acute and obtuse angles to a suitable degree of accuracy	Reason
23	Fixing points (ITP): measuring polygons	35	Understanding shape	Measure acute and obtuse angles using a protractor	Refresh

Highlighted text indicates the end-of-year objectives

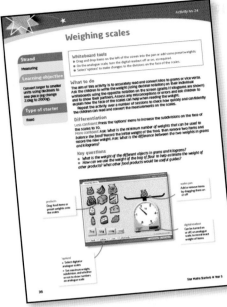

Activity pages

Each page of teachers' notes includes:

Learning objectives
Covering the strands and objectives of the renewed *Primary Framework for Mathematics*

Type of starter
Identifying one or more of the 'six Rs' of oral and mental work (see page 7)

Whiteboard tools
Identifying the key functions of the accompanying CD-ROM activity

What to do
Outline notes on how to administer the activity with the whole class

Differentiation
Adapting the activity for more or less confident learners

Key questions
Probing questions to stimulate and sustain the oral and mental work

Annotations
At-a-glance instructions for using the CD-ROM activity.

Whiteboard hints and tips

Each title offers some general support identifying practical mathematical activities that can be performed on any interactive whiteboard (see pages 8–9).

Recording sheets

Two recording sheets have been included to support your planning:
- Planning for the six Rs: plan a balance of activities across the six Rs of mental and oral maths (see page 7).
- Star Maths Starters diary: build a record of the starters used (titles, objectives covered, how they were used and dates they were used).

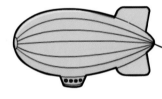

WELL DONE!

About the CD-ROM

Types of activity

Each CD-ROM contains 30 interactive starter activities for use on any interactive whiteboard. These include:

Interactive whiteboard resources
A set of engaging interactive activities specifically designed for *Star Maths Starters*. The teachers' notes on pages 13–42 of this book explain how each activity can be used for a ten-minute mental maths starter, with annotated screen shots giving you at-a-glance support. Similarly, a 'what to do' function within each activity provides at-the-board support.

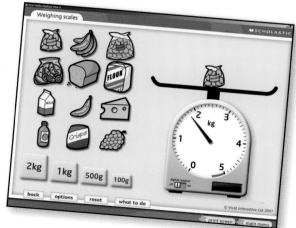

Interactive teaching programs (ITPs)

A small number of ITPs, originally developed by the National Numeracy Strategy, has been included on each CD-ROM. They are simple programs that model a range of objectives, such as data presentation or fraction bars. Their strength is that they are easy to read and use. If you press the Esc button the ITP will reduce to a window on the computer screen. It can then be enlarged or more ITPs can be launched and set up to model further objectives, or simply to extend the objective from that starter. To view the relevant 'what to do' notes once an ITP is open, press the Esc button to gain access to the function on the opening screen of the activity.

Interactive 'notepad'

A pop-up 'notepad' is built into a variety of activities. This allows the user to write answers or keep a record of workings out and includes 'pen', 'eraser' and 'clear' tools.

Teacher zone

This teachers' section includes links from the interactive activities to the *Primary Framework for Mathematics* strands, together with editable objectives grids, planning grids and printable versions of the activity sheets on pages 43–46.

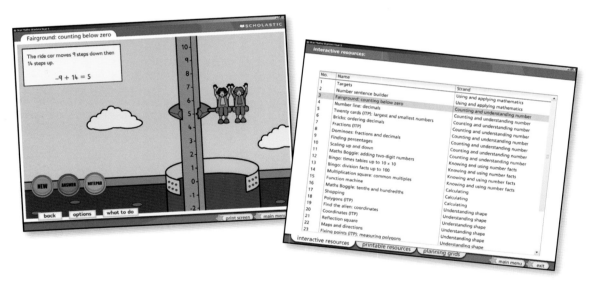

How to use the CD-ROM

System requirements

Minimum specification
- PC with a CD-ROM drive and 512 Mb RAM (recommended)
- Windows 98SE or above/Mac OSX.1 or above
- Recommended minimum processor speed: 1 GHz

Getting started

The *Star Maths Starters* CD-ROM should auto run when inserted into your CD drive. If it does not, use **My Computer** to browse the contents of the CD-ROM and click on the 'Star Maths Starters' icon.

From the start-up screen you will find four options: select **Credits** to view a list of credits. Click on **Register** to register the product to receive product updates and special offers. Click on **How to use** to access support notes for using the CD-ROM. Finally, if you agree to the terms and conditions, select **Start** to move to the main menu.

For all technical support queries, please phone Scholastic Customer Services on 0845 6039091.

The six Rs of oral and mental work

In the guidance paper *Renewing the Primary Framework for mathematics* (2006), the Primary National Strategy identified six features of children's mathematical learning that oral and mental work can support. The description of the learning and an outline of possible activities are given below:

Six Rs	Learning focus	Possible activities
Rehearse	To practise and consolidate existing skills, usually mental calculation skills, set in a context to involve children in problem solving through the use and application of these skills; use of vocabulary and language of number, properties of shapes or describing and reasoning.	Interpret words such as more, less, sum, altogether, difference, subtract; find missing numbers or missing angles on a straight line; say the number of days in four weeks or the number of 5p coins that make up 35p; describe part-revealed shapes, hidden solids; describe patterns or relationships; explain decisions or why something meets criteria.
Recall	To secure knowledge of facts, usually number facts; build up speed and accuracy; recall quickly names and properties of shapes, units of measure or types of charts, graphs to represent data.	Count on and back in steps of constant size; recite the 6-times table and derive associated division facts; name a shape with five sides or a solid with five flat faces; list properties of cuboids; state units of time and their relationships.
Refresh	To draw on and revisit previous learning; to assess, review and strengthen children's previously acquired knowledge and skills relevant to later learning; return to aspects of mathematics with which the children have had difficulty; draw out key points from learning.	Refresh multiplication facts or properties of shapes and associated vocabulary; find factor pairs for given multiples; return to earlier work on identifying fractional parts of given shapes; locate shapes in a grid as preparation for lesson on coordinates; refer to general cases and identify new cases.
Refine	To sharpen methods and procedures; explain strategies and solutions; extend ideas and develop and deepen the children's knowledge; reinforce their understanding of key concepts; build on earlier learning so that strategies and techniques become more efficient and precise.	Find differences between two two-digit numbers, extend to three-digit numbers to develop skill; find 10% of quantities, then 5% and 20% by halving and doubling; use audible and quiet counting techniques to extend skills; give coordinates of shapes in different orientations to hone concept; review informal calculation strategies.
Read	To use mathematical vocabulary and interpret images, diagrams and symbols correctly; read number sentences and provide equivalents; describe and explain diagrams and features involving scales, tables or graphs; identify shapes from a list of their properties; read and interpret word problems and puzzles; create their own problems and lines of enquiry.	Tell a story using an interactive bar chart; alter the chart for children to retell the story; starting with a number sentence (eg 2 + 11 = 13), children generate and read equivalent statements for 13; read values on scales with different intervals; read information about a shape and eliminate possible shapes; set number sentences in given contexts; read others' results and offer new questions and ideas for enquiry.
Reason	To use and apply acquired knowledge, skills and understanding; make informed choices and decisions, predict and hypothesise; use deductive reasoning to eliminate or conclude; provide examples that satisfy a condition always, sometimes or never and say why.	Sort shapes into groups and give reasons for selection; discuss why alternative methods of calculation work and when to use them; decide what calculation to do in a problem and explain the choice; deduce a solid from a 2D picture; use fractions to express proportions; draw conclusions from given statements to solve puzzles.

Each one of the styles of starter enables children to access different mathematical skills and each has a different outcome, as identified above. A bingo game, for example, provides a good way of rehearsing number facts, whereas a 'scales' activity supports reading skills. In the objectives grid on pages 10-11, the type of each Star Starters activity is identified to make it easier to choose appropriate styles of starter matched to a particular objective. A 'Six Rs' recording sheet has also been provided on page 12 (with an editable version on the CD-ROM) to track the types of starter you will be using against the strands of the renewed Framework.

Using the interactive whiteboard in primary mathematics

The interactive whiteboard is an invaluable tool for teaching and learning mathematics. It can be used to demonstrate and model mathematical concepts to the whole class, offering the potential to share children's learning experiences. It gives access to powerful resources – audio, video, images, websites and interactive activities – to discuss, interact with and learn from. *Star Maths Starters* provides 30 quality interactive resources that are easy to set up and use and which help children to improve their mathematical development and thinking skills through their use as short, focused oral and mental starters.

Whiteboard resources and children's learning

There are many reasons why the whiteboard, especially in mathematics, enhances children's learning:

- Using high-quality interactive maths resources will engage children in the process of learning and developing their mathematical thinking skills. Resources such as maths games can create a real sense of theatre in the whole class and promote a real desire to achieve and succeed in a task.
- As mentioned above, the whiteboard can be used to demonstrate some very important mathematical concepts. For example, many teachers find that children understand place value much faster and more thoroughly through using interactive resources on a whiteboard. Similarly, the whiteboard can support children's visualisation of mathematics, especially for 'Shape and Space' activities.
- Although mathematics usually has a correct or incorrect answer, there are often several ways of reaching the same result. The whiteboard allows the teacher to demonstrate methods and encourages children to present and compare their own mental or written methods of calculation.

Using a whiteboard in Year 5

An interactive whiteboard can be used for a variety of purposes in Year 5 mathematics lessons. These include:

- demonstrating fractions of shapes or equivalent fractions using diagrams or clip art; shapes and objects can also be used to show the relationship between fractions and division;
- ordering fractions or decimals on a number line;
- using the whiteboard to demonstrate or check children's understanding of written methods of calculation;
- using calculators to demonstrate different functions or to show number patterns, such as sequences of negative numbers;
- involving the whole class in identifying line symmetry in shapes, patterns or objects such as the letters of the alphabet, butterflies, rangoli patterns;
- using software to teach the 'data-handling cycle': start with a question, collect data, process and present the data on the whiteboard, ask the whole class to interpret the data and answer questions about it.

Practical considerations

For the teacher, the whiteboard has the potential to save preparation and classroom time, as well as providing more flexible teaching.

ICT resources for the interactive whiteboard often involve numbers that are randomly generated, so that possible questions or calculations stemming from a single resource may be many and varied. This enables resources to be used for a longer or shorter time period depending on the purpose of the activity and how children's learning is progressing. *Star Maths Starters* includes many activities of this type.

From the very practical point of view of saving teachers' time, particularly in the starter activity, it is often easier to set up mathematics resources more quickly than those for other subjects. Once the software is familiar, preparation time is saved especially when there is need for clear presentation, as in drawing shapes accurately or creating charts and diagrams for 'Handling data' activities.

Maths resources on the interactive whiteboard are often flexible and enable differentiation so that a teacher can access different degrees of difficulty using the same software. Last but not least, whiteboard resources save time writing on the board and software often checks calculations, if required, which enables more time both for teaching and assessing children's understanding.

Using *Star Maths Starters* interactively

Much has been said and written about interactivity in the classroom but it is not always clear what this means. For example, children coming out to the board and ticking a box is not what is meant by 'whole-class interactive teaching and learning'. In mathematics it is about challenging children's ideas so that they develop their own thinking skills and, when appropriate, encouraging them to make connections across different mathematical topics. As a teacher, this means asking suitable questions and encouraging children to explore and discuss their methods of calculation and whether there are alternative ways of achieving the same result. *Star Maths Starters* provides some examples of key questions that could be asked while the activities are being undertaken, together with suggestions for how to engage less confident learners and stretch the more confident.

If you already have some experience in using the whiteboard interactively then we hope the teaching suggestions set out in this book will take you further. What is especially important is the facility the whiteboard provides to share pupils' mathematical learning experiences. This does not mean just asking children to suggest answers, but using the facility of the board to display and discuss ideas so that everyone can share in the learning experience. Obviously, this needs to be in a way that explores and relates the thinking of individuals to the context of the learning that is happening.

In the best whiteboard classrooms, teachers comment that the board provides a shared learning experience between the teacher and the class, in so far as the teacher may sometimes stand aside while children themselves are discussing their own mathematical methods and ideas.

Starter Number	Star Starter Title	Page No.	Strand	Learning objective as taken from the Primary Framework for Mathematics	Type of Starter
1	Targets	13	Using and applying mathematics	Represent a puzzle or problem by identifying and recording the information or calculations needed to solve it	Reason
2	Number sentence builder	14	Using and applying mathematics	Represent a puzzle or problem by identifying and recording the information or calculations needed to solve it	Reason
3	Fairground: counting below zero	15	Counting and understanding number	Count from any given number in whole-number steps, extending beyond zero when counting backwards; relate the numbers to their position on a number line	Recall
4	Number line: decimals	16	Counting and understanding number	Count from any given number in whole-number and decimal steps; relate the numbers to their position on a number line	Refine
5	Twenty cards (ITP): largest and smallest numbers	17	Counting and understanding number	Explain what each digit represents in whole numbers	Reason
6	Bricks: ordering decimals	18	Counting and understanding number	Explain what each digit represents in whole numbers and decimals with up to two places	Reason
7	Fractions (ITP)	19	Counting and understanding number	Relate fractions to their decimal representations	Refresh
8	Dominoes: fractions and decimals	20	Counting and understanding number	Relate fractions to their decimal representations	Refresh
9	Finding percentages	21	Counting and understanding number	Understand percentage as the number of parts in every 100 and express tenths and hundredths as percentages	Refine
10	Scaling up and down	22	Counting and understanding number	Use sequences to scale numbers up or down; solve problems involving proportions of quantities	Read
11	Maths Boggle: adding two-digit numbers	23	Knowing and using number facts	Use knowledge of place value and addition and subtraction of two-digit numbers to derive sums	Refine
12	Bingo: times tables up to 10 × 10	24	Knowing and using number facts	Recall quickly multiplication facts up to 10 × 10	Rehearse
13	Bingo: division facts up to 100	25	Knowing and using number facts	Identify pairs of factors of two-digit whole numbers	Rehearse
14	Multiplication square: common multiples	26	Knowing and using number facts	Identify pairs of factors of two-digit whole numbers and find common multiples	Read
15	Function machine	27	Calculating	Use efficient written methods to add and subtract whole numbers	Reason

Starter Number	Star Starter Title	Page No.	Strand	Learning objective as taken from the Primary Framework for Mathematics	Type of Starter
16	Maths Boggle: tenths and hundredths	28	Calculating	Use efficient written methods to add and subtract whole numbers and decimals with up to two places	Refine
17	Shopping	29	Calculating	Use efficient written methods to add and subtract whole numbers and decimals with up to two places	Refine
18	Polygons (ITP)	30	Understanding shape	Identify, visualise and describe properties of rectangles, triangles and regular polygons	Refresh
19	Find the alien: coordinates	31	Understanding shape	Read and plot coordinates in the first quadrant	Reason
20	Coordinates (ITP)	32	Understanding shape	Read and plot coordinates in the first quadrant	Refine
21	Reflection square	33	Understanding shape	Complete patterns with up to two lines of symmetry; draw the position of a shape after a reflection	Refine
22	Maps and directions	34	Understanding shape	Estimate acute and obtuse angles to a suitable degree of accuracy	Reason
23	Fixing points (ITP): measuring polygons	35	Understanding shape	Measure acute and obtuse angles using a protractor	Refresh
24	Weighing scales	36	Measuring	Convert larger to smaller units using decimals to one place (eg change 2.6kg to 2600g)	Read
25	Thermometer (ITP)	37	Measuring	Interpret a reading that lies between two unnumbered divisions on a scale	Read
26	Measuring jug	38	Measuring	Interpret a reading that lies between two unnumbered divisions on a scale	Refine
27	Ruler (ITP)	39	Measuring	Draw and measure lines to the nearest millimetre	Refine
28	Area (ITP)	40	Measuring	Measure and calculate the perimeter of regular and irregular polygons	Rehearse
29	Clocks: time difference using 24-hour time	41	Measuring	Read time using 24-hour clock notation	Read
30	Data handling (ITP)	42	Handling data	Answer a set of questions by collecting, selecting and organising relevant data; use ICT to present features	Read

Planning for the six Rs of oral and mental work

Oral and mental activity – six Rs	Using and applying mathematics	Counting and understanding number	Knowing and using number facts	Calculating	Understanding shape	Measuring	Handling data
Rehearse			● Bingo: times tables up to 10 × 10 ● Bingo: division facts up to 100			● Area (ITP)	
Recall		● Fairground: counting below zero					
Refresh		● Fractions (ITP) ● Dominoes: fractions and decimals			● Polygons (ITP) ● Fixing points (ITP); measuring polygons		
Refine		● Number line: decimals ● Finding percentages	● Maths Boggle: adding two-digit numbers	● Maths Boggle: tenths and hundredths ● Shopping	● Coordinates (ITP) ● Reflection square	● Measuring jug ● Ruler (ITP)	
Read		● Scaling up and down	● Multiplication square: common multiples			● Weighing scales ● Thermometer (ITP) ● Clocks: time difference using 24-hour time	● Data handling (ITP)
Reason	● Targets ● Number sentence builder	● Twenty cards (ITP): largest and smallest numbers ● Bricks: ordering decimals		● Function machine	● Find the alien: coordinates ● Maps and directions		

Targets

Strand

Using and applying mathematics

Learning objective

Represent a puzzle or problem by identifying and recording the information or calculations needed to solve it

Type of starter

Reason

Whiteboard tools

● Press 'go' to generate five number cards.
● In 'options' select 'randomly generated' in order for the program to generate a target number, or select 'entered by teacher' to manually insert a number into the target.
● Use the 'notepad' to work out calculations. A pen tool will automatically pop up when the notepad opens. Press 'start again' or the 'eraser' to delete any text.
● Press 'winner' if the children complete the activity successfully.

What to do

The aim of this activity is for children to use known number facts to find a target number. Once five cards have been generated, select a target number that is achievable with the numbers shown and type it into the target. In 'random mode' the target number will be generated automatically. Encourage the children to use known strategies in order to write number sentences that match (or nearly match) the target number. Invite individual children to write their calculations on the 'notepad' and review the process. At this point, encourage the rest of the class to challenge the process or calculations used – or suggest an alternative method.

Differentiation

Less confident: at this age, children should be encouraged to use all four standard number operations (+, −, × and ÷), though you might initially limit the activity to addition and subtraction facts. For additional support provide each child with a copy of the photocopiable 'Targets' sheet on page 43.
More confident: encourage the children to use simple squared numbers (for example, $5^2 \times 5 = 125$). Ask questions such as: Would the target be achieved faster using this method? Why?

Key questions

● What strategies are the most efficient? How do they help you to 'hit the target'?
● What tips would you give somebody who was new to the game?

'go'
Press to generate five number cards

'options'
Select 'randomly generated' or 'entered by teacher' for target number

'winner'
Press when target answer is found

'notepad'
Note calculations here using pen tool

Number sentence builder

Strand

Using and applying mathematics

Learning objective

Represent a puzzle or problem by identifying and recording the information or calculations needed to solve it

Type of starter

Reason

Whiteboard tools
● Move cards and symbols onto the line to build a number sentence.
● Drag and drop numbers and symbols within a line to re-order them.
● Drag cards off the line to remove them.
● Press 'reset' to start again.

What to do

The aim of the activity is to find the unknown number or numbers represented by symbols in a number sentence so that both sides of the equals (=) sign balance. Numbers of any size can be selected, as two digits selected consecutively snap together to form a two-digit number, three digits form a three-digit number, and so on. For Year 5 use numbers up to 100 in order to tease out the logic and understanding of how to find the missing number rather than asking the children to complete complex calculations.

Try to prepare number sentences that have more than one possible solution. For example: in solving $2 \times \square \times \triangle = 40$, $\triangle$ and $\square$ could be different numbers whose product is 20.

Differentiation

Less confident: start with simple straightforward sentences such as $3 \times 10 = \square$ until children get used to the idea that the symbol represents a number.
More confident: ask children to make up their own number sentences to challenge the whole class. They may quickly learn that it is not always quite as easy as it looks, as more than one solution is often possible.

Key questions

● *What is the missing number (or numbers), and are there any other numbers that might work?*
● *Are there any number sentences using addition and subtraction that don't always work?*

number sentence
Drag numbers and symbols to re-order

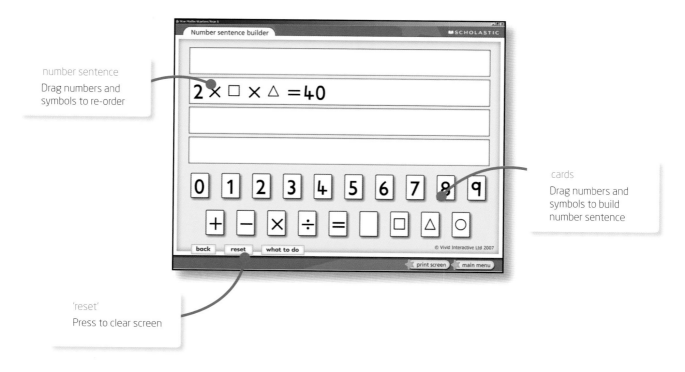

cards
Drag numbers and symbols to build number sentence

'reset'
Press to clear screen

Fairground: counting below zero

Strand

Counting and understanding number

Learning objective

Count from any given number in whole-number steps, extending beyond zero when counting backwards; relate the numbers to their position on a number line

Type of starter

Recall

Whiteboard tools
- Start point: the riders start at ground level or zero.
- Move the riders up and down the ride in steps of 1 to solve a maths problem or number sentence.
- Use the 'notepad' to show calculations.
- Press 'new' to move the riders back to the starting point and to generate a new question.

What to do

Use this activity to encourage the children to add or subtract mentally in steps of 1 when the number line extends below zero. Encourage them to use their individual whiteboards so that they can work out the answers for themselves prior to any class discussion. Extend the activity beyond the initial question by asking, for example: *What would happen if the riders now move down another 4 steps?* Illustrate this by dragging and dropping the riders to the new position. Invite children to come to the board to use the on-screen notepad to show their calculations.

Differentiation

Less confident: support the children with the photocopiable 'Fairground: counting below zero' sheet on page 44, by setting some questions with the riders always starting at zero.
More confident: ask children what they think would happen if the riders move off the vertical scale shown.

Key questions
- *On which number do the riders end up? How do you know?*
- *From −6, how far up the ride would the riders need to climb to reach step 5?*

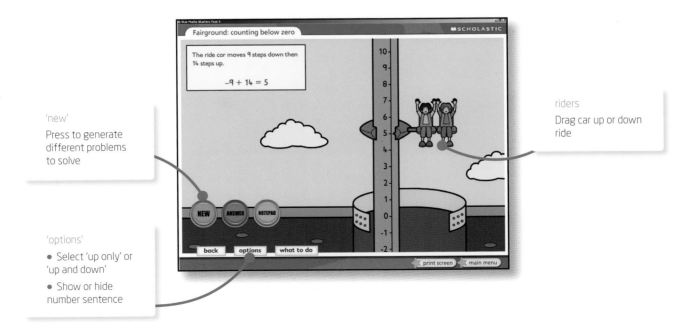

'new'
Press to generate different problems to solve

The ride car moves 9 steps down then 14 steps up.

$$-9 + 14 = 5$$

riders
Drag car up or down ride

'options'
- Select 'up only' or 'up and down'
- Show or hide number sentence

Number line: decimals

Strand

Counting and understanding number

Learning objective

Count from any given number in whole-number and decimal steps; relate the numbers to their position on a number line

Type of starter

Refine

Whiteboard tools

● Select options: under 'start number' select 20, under 'end number' select 40, under 'step' select 1, and under 'subdivisions' select 10.
● Drag the red pointer across the number line to position it.
● Drag the red green pointer across the number line to position it.
● Hide the values of the red and green marker numbers using the 'options' button.

What to do

Move the red marker to a decimal number close to the starting point and ask the children to read the number. Discuss what the next number will be if counting up in ones. Then ask the children to count up in steps of 2 or 3 from the starting point. In a similar way, drag the green marker to a decimal number close to the end number and ask the children to count down in different steps from the number on the green marker. The starting and finishing points can easily be altered using the options buttons though the scale may become difficult to read if the difference between the start and end points is more than about 20.

Differentiation

Less confident: move the markers to whole numbers at first until they are more confident.
More confident: drag and drop both pointers and ask children to find the difference between the two numbers.

Key questions

● *What would the new number be if 10, 11 or 12… is added to the red marker number?*
● *What would the new number be if 10, 11 or 12… is subtracted from the green marker number?*

'options'
● Start at a different whole number
● Hide marker values

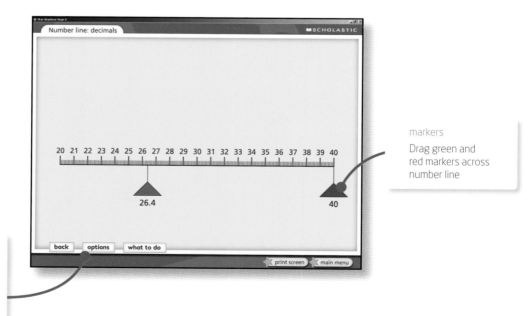

markers
Drag green and red markers across number line

Twenty cards (ITP): largest and smallest numbers

Strand

Counting and understanding number

Learning objective

Explain what each digit represents in whole numbers

Type of starter

Reason

Whiteboard tools
- Press the pack of cards with the blue outline and select 'random numbers' from the menu.
- Move the arrow to the right of 'How many cards' to 4.
- Move the arrow to the right of 'Maximum number' to 9.
- Leave 'Minimum number' at zero.
- Press 'go'.
- Four cards will be stacked up which can be dragged and dropped to the middle of the screen.
- Press the red part of a card to reveal each number.
- Drag the cards by their centres to re-arrange them in order.

What to do
Tell the children that the aim of this activity is to make the largest and smallest numbers possible using the four cards. Press 'go' to select four cards from the pack at random. Ask the children to write the largest numbers possible using these four numbers on their individual whiteboards. Re-arrange the cards on the board and question the children about why they decided on a particular arrangement of the cards. Prompt for understanding using language such as *the thousands place, the hundreds place* and so on. By using eight cards this number game can be played in a similar way with two teams, although of course there is an element of chance involved. Alternatively, play the game with the whole class, revealing only one number and putting it into place before revealing the 2nd, 3rd and 4th.

Differentiation
Less confident: invite the children to make the largest and smallest number by revealing all the numbers on the cards at the start.
More confident: ask the children if they can think of any strategies that might help them create the largest number when just one number has been revealed.

Key questions
- If the first card is 0 or 1, where would you place it to make the largest/smallest number?
- If the number on the first card is 8 or 9, where would you position it to make the largest/smallest number?

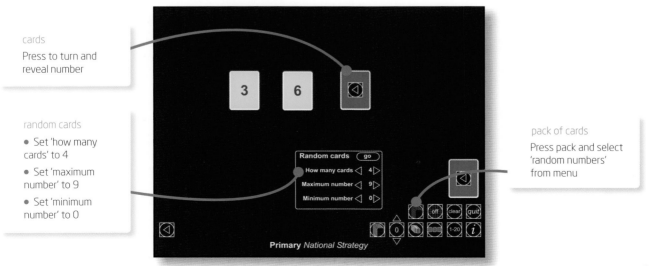

cards
Press to turn and reveal number

random cards
- Set 'how many cards' to 4
- Set 'maximum number' to 9
- Set 'minimum number' to 0

pack of cards
Press pack and select 'random numbers' from menu

Bricks: ordering decimals

Strand

Counting and understanding number

Learning objective

Explain what each digit represents in whole numbers and decimals with up to two places

Type of starter

Reason

Whiteboard tools
- Use the options to fix the first digit of the numbers, if required.
- Press 'go' to generate five bricks each showing a number between 0 and 10 with two decimal places.
- Drag each brick into the gaps in the wall, with the smallest number in the lowest position, to complete the wall.
- If all five bricks are positioned correctly, a 'Well done' message appears. If any bricks are placed incorrectly, a 'Try again' message appears. Press 'ok' and the bricks move back to their starting position.
- Press 'go' again to select a new set of bricks.

What to do
Use this activity either to rehearse existing strategies for ordering decimals or to probe children's reasoning. Press 'go' to reveal five bricks, each showing a number between 0 and 10 with two decimal places. Ask the children to work as a whole class to decide the correct order, writing answers on their individual whiteboards. Position the bricks in the wall by dragging and dropping them, or ask individual children to place them.

Differentiation
Less confident: use a number line to support the children's ordering skills before positioning the bricks in the wall. Fix the first digit to limit the number range.
More confident: ask the children what would need to be added to the top brick to make 10.

Key questions
- *What does the number to the right/left of the decimal point represent on each brick?*
- *What would the new number be if 1, 2 or 3... is added to the number on the lowest brick?*

bricks
Order by dragging into wall

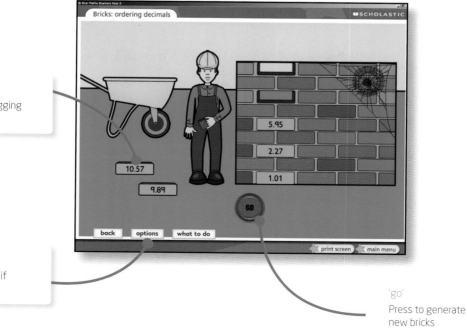

'options'
Fix first digit if required

'go'
Press to generate new bricks

Fractions (ITP)

Whiteboard tools
- Press the small green and yellow bar to produce fraction bars, up to a maximum of five.
- Press the arrows next to the fraction bar to increase or decrease the denominator, in steps of 1, and show the fraction chosen.
- Press 'fdpr' to reveal the fractions, decimals, percentages and ratios equivalent to each bar.
- Press the individual fractions on each 'fractions bar' to change the colours from green to yellow to create different fractions on screen.
- Press 'reset' to clear all but the lowest green bar.

What to do

The aim of this starter is to identify corresponding fractions in order to create a whole number. Start with four bars on the screen partitioned into $\frac{1}{2}$, $\frac{1}{4}$, $\frac{1}{8}$ and $\frac{1}{16}$. Change one section of each to yellow and ask the class what the corresponding fraction would be in order to make a whole (for example, $\frac{3}{4}$ would need to be highlighted to complete the quarter bar). Next ask: *How could we make each bar equivalent to $\frac{1}{2}$? How can this be demonstrated?* Use the 'fdpr' button, selecting the D (decimals), to show that when the appropriate sections are highlighted in yellow, each bar has the same decimal (in this case 0.5). Reset the bars and select a new target. It might be useful to show a fraction that cannot have the same equivalence. Ask: *How close is its decimal representation to the equivalent fraction?*

Differentiation

Less confident: review common fractions and use the bars to demonstrate equivalence.
More confident: translate the fractions to percentages in order to make 100%.

Key questions

- *How do the bars help you to 'see' the fractions?*
- *Who can identify an equivalent fraction?* (Ask individual children to come to the board to demonstrate.)

fraction bar
Press to change from green to yellow

denominator
Press arrows to change denominator

add fraction bars
Press to produce up to five fraction bars

fdpr
Press to show fractions, decimals, percentages and ratios equivalent to each bar

Dominoes: fractions and decimals

Strand

Counting and understanding number

Learning objective

Relate fractions to their decimal representations

Type of starter

Refresh

Whiteboard tools

- Press 'new' to start a new game.
- Press the 'miss a go' button to take another domino from the pot.
- Domino:
  - Drag and drop into the game.
  - Press to rotate 90˚.
- Press 'winner' if Player 1 or Player 2 has placed all of the dominoes.

What to do

The aim of this activity is to match domino fractions with the equivalent domino decimals. The game is played in the same way as regular dominoes with two groups playing against each other. Each group or 'player' (maximum of two) is dealt five dominoes. A starter domino is selected by the computer to begin the game and the players then take turns to play. If a player is unable to place a domino they must take one from the central pot. Play continues until a player places all of their dominoes, and is declared the winner, or there are no dominoes left in the pot. If a stalemate situation is created, in which neither player can play a domino and the pot is empty, the player with fewest remaining dominoes is the winner.

Differentiation

Less confident: use 'talk partners' to discuss moves, which will help to support a child's confidence and affirm their decisions.
More confident: play 'beat the teacher', in which children attempt to pit themselves against an adult in the classroom.

Key questions

- *What methods did you use to identify which dominoes to select?*
- *What strategies would you use in order to block your opponent?*

domino
- Drag domino to playing space
- Rotate by pressing top right-hand corner

players 1 and 2
Panel turns green to indicate whose turn it is

'miss a go'
Press to take another domino from pot

'new'
Press to start new game

Finding percentages

Strand

Counting and understanding number

Learning objective

Understand percentage as the number of parts in every 100 and express tenths and hundredths as percentages

Type of starter

Refine

Whiteboard tools
- Highlight a number of squares on the blank 10 × 10 grid.
- Press 'clear' to start again.

What to do
Highlight ten squares,s then ask the children how many squares have been selected out of 100. Using their individual whiteboards, tell them to write this down as a fraction out of 100 ($^1/_{10}$). Then ask them to write this down as a percentage (10%). If necessary, remind the class that 'per cent' means 'parts in every 100'. Next, select a whole number of columns (for example, 5)and ask the children to write this down as a fraction out of 100, a percentage, and as a fraction out of 10. Develop the activity by asking the children to come to the board to shade 50% of the grid. Extend to other fractions and percentages.

Differentiation
Less confident: start by highlighting a small number of squares only until children understand the concept of a percentage.
More confident: by shading in appropriate squares, ask children if they can express 50%, 25%, 20%, and so on, as fractions.

Key questions
- *How many parts out of 100 have been shaded?*
- *What percentage is this?*

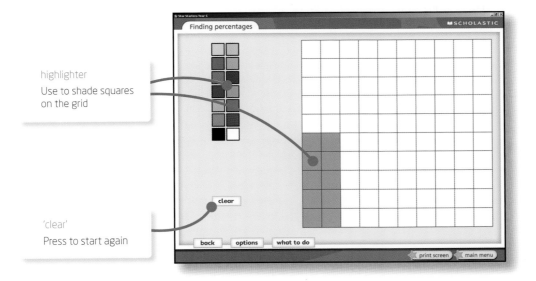

highlighter
Use to shade squares on the grid

'clear'
Press to start again

Scaling up and down

Strand

Counting and understanding number

Learning objective

Use sequences to scale numbers up or down; solve problems involving proportions of quantities

Type of starter

Read

Whiteboard tools

- Select the number of beads required from the 'options' menu.
- Choose different colours from the palette and build up a pattern.
- If a colour needs to be removed, press the white bead.
- Press 'clear' to start again.

What to do

Create a pattern of beads using two or three colours. Note that to fit the bead length chosen, the number of beads used in the pattern must divide into the bead length used with no remainder. So, for example, if the length of beads chosen is 18, the pattern should use two, three, six or nine beads. Ask the children to predict the pattern themselves and continue the pattern using squared paper. Once the pattern has been established, encourage the children to use the correct vocabulary to describe proportions. (For example: *Two out of every three beads is blue.*) Ask them to work out without counting how many of each colour there would be if the pattern length were doubled or trebled... and then illustrate this by adding the appropriate beads.

Try some patterns that are made up of multiples of 2 or 3 (for example, 6 red beads and 12 blue). Ask the children how many of each colour there would be if the proportions were decreased by 2 or by 3.

Differentiation

Less confident: use two colours only so that children get used to using the correct language and concentrate on describing the patterns and proportions accurately in the early stages of the activity.
More confident: use three colours and extend the children's vocabulary to expressing the proportions in fractions. For example: *Two thirds of the beads are green.*

Key questions

- *How would you describe this pattern?*
- *How many beads of each colour would there be if the pattern of beads is four times as long?*

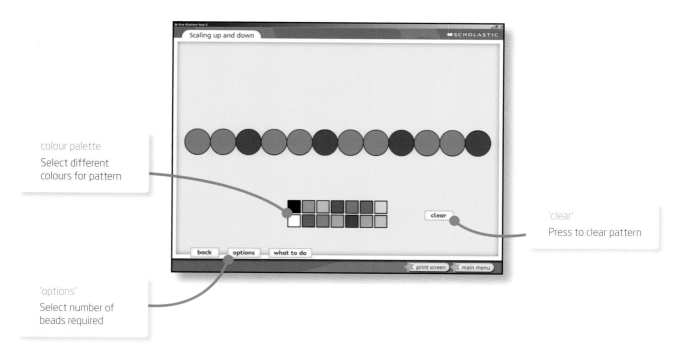

colour palette
Select different colours for pattern

'clear'
Press to clear pattern

'options'
Select number of beads required

Maths Boggle: adding two-digit numbers

23

Strand

Knowing and using number facts

Learning objective

Use knowledge of place value and addition and subtraction of two-digit numbers to derive sums

Type of starter

Refine

Whiteboard tools

● Press 'new' to rattle the Boggle dice.
● Change the target by selecting a new question from the 'options' menu.
● Highlight each dice by pressing it once (to remove the highlight, press again).
● Press 'new' for a new set of numbers.
● Use the 'notepad' to show workings out.

What to do

The aim of this activity is to use mental methods of addition and, where these are well established, to begin to use more sophisticated strategies to estimate which number string (column or row) has the target answer. In this version, the number strings are known number facts.

Start the game by selecting a question from the 'options' menu at the foot of the screen (or, should you wish, by stating your own target). Once this has been understood, the dice are 'rattled' to reveal a random selection of two-digit numbers. In pairs or individually, ask the children to answer the question by using these numbers. You can then highlight dice by pressing them. Challenge children to come to the board to show their calculations using the on-screen notepad.

Differentiation

Less confident: identify the number string that has the most multiples of one number and add those numbers.
More confident: provide some children with calculators. Ask: *Are calculators faster than mental strategies?*

Key questions

● *How do doubles speed up the adding process?*
● *What methods might you use to check answers?* (For example, finding doubles or multiples of a number, adding near doubles, identifying number bonds.)

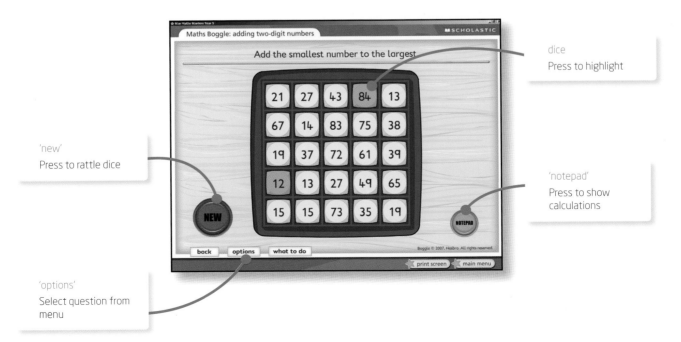

'new'
Press to rattle dice

'options'
Select question from menu

dice
Press to highlight

'notepad'
Press to show calculations

Bingo: times tables up to 10 × 10

Strand

Knowing and using number facts

Learning objective

Recall quickly multiplication facts up to 10 × 10

Type of starter

Rehearse

Whiteboard tools

● Use the 'options' menu to set the timer to adjust time between bingo calls (5-20 seconds).
● Press the 'start' button to start a new game.
● Press 'check grid' to check answers if someone calls *House*.
● Press 'play on' or 'winner' after checking a player's grid.

What to do

This activity is designed to rehearse number facts and encourage quick recall of multiples up to 10 × 10 against a time limit. Provide each child or, alternatively, each pair with a bingo card, which can be printed from the opening screen or prepared using the bingo card template on page 45.

Each ball offers a different number sentence. If the answer appears on their bingo grid, the children mark it off. If the children are new to the game, allow for a longer amount of time between bingo calls. If a child calls *House* (or other similar winning call), press 'check grid' to pause the game and call up all of the completed number sentences that have been called. If they are correct, press the 'winner' button for an appropriate fanfare or press 'play on' to continue the game.

Differentiation

Less confident: simplify the game by extending the time between questions and asking the children to call *House* after correctly identifying five answers.
More confident: increase the number of answers on the bingo cards using the bingo card template on page 45.

Key questions

● *Were any of the answers on your bingo cards the same for different questions?* (For example, 4 × 8 and 8 × 4 have the same product.) *If so, what patterns can you see in the numbers? (*For example, are they multiples of themselves or inverted?)
● *What strategies did you use to remember these multiplication facts?*

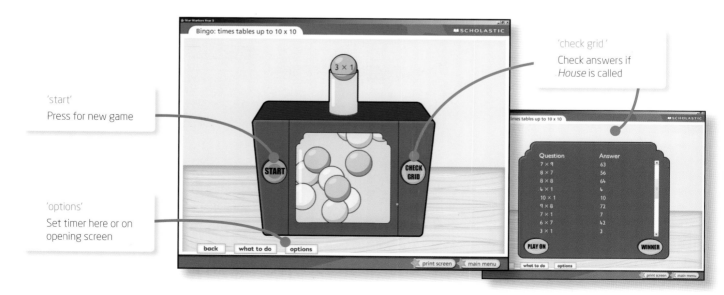

'start'
Press for new game

'options'
Set timer here or on opening screen

'check grid'
Check answers if *House* is called

Bingo: division facts up to 100

Strand

Knowing and using number facts

Learning objective

Identify pairs of factors of two-digit whole numbers

Type of starter

Rehearse

Whiteboard tools
- Use the 'options' menu to set the timer to adjust time between bingo calls (5-20 seconds).
- Press the 'start' button to start a new game.
- Press 'check grid' to check answers if someone calls *House*.
- Press 'play on' or 'winner' after checking a player's grid.

What to do

The aim of this activity is for quick recall of division facts up to 100 (for example, 24 ÷ 4 = □) against a time limit. Provide each child or, alternatively, each pair with a bingo card, which can be printed from the opening screen or prepared using the bingo card template on page 45. The children have to match the numbers called out to the ones on their grids. They can either play in pairs or individually. If the children are new to the game, allow for a longer amount of time between bingo calls. If a child calls *House* (or other similar winning call), press 'check grid' to pause the game and call up a table of all of the completed number sentences that have been called. If they are correct, press the 'winner' button for an appropriate fanfare or press 'play on' to continue the game.

Differentiation

Less confident: if time is limited, ask children to call *House* once they have correctly paired five numbers (or however many you feel time allows).
More confident: increase the total of numbers on the bingo card using the bingo card template on page 45.

Key questions
- *How can you prove that you have all the correct answers without referring to the answer display?*
- *What strategies did you use to remember these division facts?*

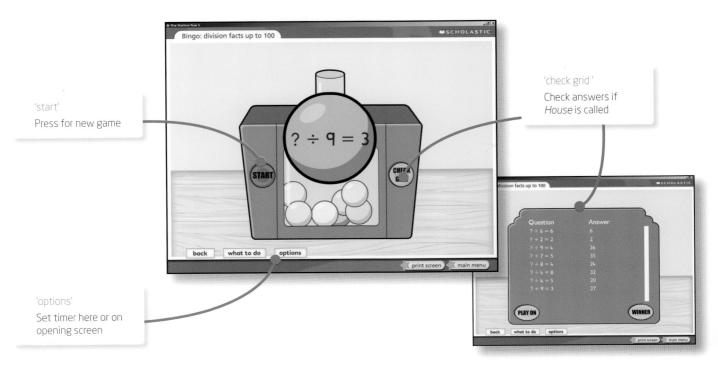

'start'
Press for new game

'check grid'
Check answers if *House* is called

'options'
Set timer here or on opening screen

Multiplication square: common multiples

Strand

Knowing and using number facts

Learning objective

Identify pairs of factors of two-digit whole numbers and find common multiples

Type of starter

Read

Whiteboard tools

- Press any square to highlight the number.
- Use the 'hide' button to hide one of the numbers on the grid.
- Select 'clear' and then press any hidden square to reveal the number beneath.
- Select 'reset' to remove all highlighting or hidden numbers.

What to do

Ask the children to look for squares in which the same number appears in different parts of the table (for example, 18) and highlight those squares on the multiplication square. (Exclude numbers that are 1 times itself.) Remind the children that 18 is a common multiple of 2, 3, 6 and 9. Using their individual whiteboards, ask the children to write down the multiplication number sentences relating to the number 18: $18 = 2 \times 9$, $18 = 3 \times 6$, $18 = 6 \times 3$, $18 = 9 \times 2$. Explain that 2 and 9, and 3 and 6, are pairs of factors of 18. Ask the children to use their whiteboards to find other common multiples (for example, 20), and check their answers on the interactive multiplication square.

Differentiation

Less confident: concentrate on the meaning of a multiple before moving on to the meaning of common multiples.
More confident: ask children to find all the common multiples of, for example, 6 and 9 and tell you what they discover.

Key questions

- *Can you explain what the word 'multiple' means?*
- *Are there any other common multiples of 2, 3, 6 and 9? How do you know?*

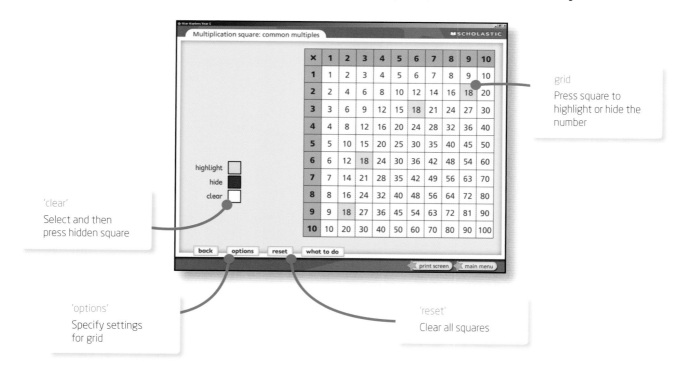

grid
Press square to highlight or hide the number

'clear'
Select and then press hidden square

'options'
Specify settings for grid

'reset'
Clear all squares

Function machine

Strand

Calculating

Learning objective

Use efficient written methods to add and subtract whole numbers

Type of starter

Reason

Whiteboard tools

- Use the 'options' menu to set the 'machine mode'. Select from 'manual' or 'random' options.
- Select 'manual' to prepare your own number sentences, or 'random' to produce a computer-generated number sentence.
- Use the pop-up keypad which appears when you press on a window to enter a number.
- Press the 'history' button to view a list of the number sentences completed during the lesson.

What to do

The aim of this activity is to find missing two- or three-digit numbers or the function in order to complete a number sentence. Either the teacher or the computer can generate these using either the 'random' or 'manual' mode options.

Manual mode: Enter some number sentences involving the addition or subtraction of pairs of numbers (for example, 210 + 119, 455 – 193 and so on). Use the drop-down menu in the function window to select either a + or – operation. Press 'go' to check answers.

Random mode: The computer selects a number sentence, but hides the input, output and function windows on the machine. Decide which element to reveal first and press that window to open it. After one other element has been revealed, ask the children to write down and then display the missing number or function. Check their answers and then press 'go' to check the answer on the machine.

Sequences can be demonstrated using the machine. For example, adding 20 to a number can be modelled by keeping the function to +20 and keying the created output number back into the input, thereby adding 20 to the number each time. A record of this will be kept in the 'history' option.

Differentiation

Less confident: work in 'manual' mode and limit the number range as required.
More confident: ask children to demonstrate the written calculations they used to answer each question.

Key questions

- *How did you work out the missing part of the sentence?*
- *How much of the sentence needs to be revealed before you can complete it?*

'new'
- Press to start again in 'manual' mode
- Press for number sentence in 'random' mode

'options'
- Select 'manual mode' to enter your own numbers
- Select 'random mode' for computer-generated numbers, initially hidden

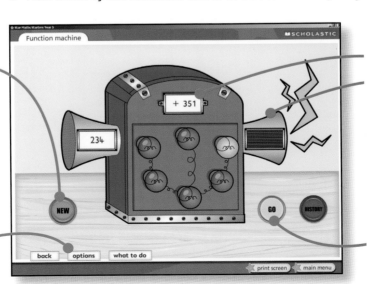

windows
- Type numbers and functions in 'manual' mode
- Press to open in 'random' mode.

'go'
Press to check answer

Maths Boggle: tenths and hundredths

Strand

Calculating

Learning objective

Use efficient written methods to add and subtract whole numbers and decimals with up to two places

Type of starter

Refine

Whiteboard tools
● Press 'new' to rattle the Boggle dice.
● Select questions from the 'options' menu.
● Highlight each dice by pressing it once (to remove the highlight, press again).
● Press 'new' for a new set of numbers.
● Use the 'notepad' to show workings out.

What to do

The aim of this activity is to use mental methods of addition and, where this is well established, to begin to use more sophisticated strategies to estimate, then calculate, answers to a set of prepared questions. In this version, the questions relate to decimal number strings (for example, adding rows and columns).

Start the game by selecting a question from the 'options' menu at the foot of the screen (or, should you wish, by stating your own target). Once this has been understood, the dice are 'rattled' to reveal a random selection of numbers. In pairs or individually, the children set out to answer the question by using these numbers. Check answers before pressing the relevant dice to highlight them. Challenge children to come to the board to show their calculations using the on-screen notepad.

Differentiation

Less confident: use a limited range of questions (for example, adding the four corners). Focus on children's methods of adding the decimals, in particular adding decimals with a total of 10.

More confident: ask pairs of children to think of their own questions for their partners to answer.

Key questions
● *If you know that 0.7 + 0.6 = 1.3, what other facts do you know?*
● *What methods might you use to check answers?* (For example, finding doubles or multiples of a number, adding near doubles, adding decimals with a total of 1 or 10.)

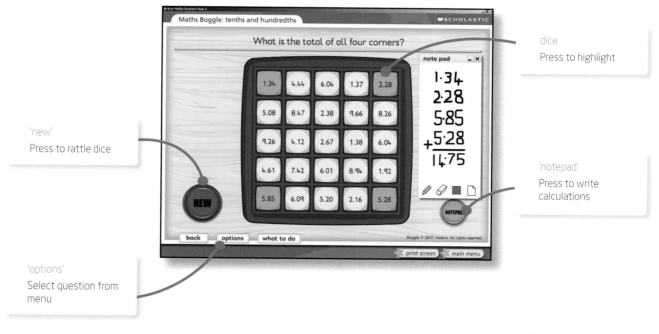

dice
Press to highlight

'new'
Press to rattle dice

'notepad'
Press to write calculations

'options'
Select question from menu

Shopping

Strand

Calculating

Learning objective

Use efficient written methods to add and subtract whole numbers and decimals with up to two decimal places

Type of starter

Refine

Whiteboard tools

- Drag one item from the shop into the shopping basket.
- Press 'check-out' to take the basket to the till on the next screen.
- Press one of the pink buttons on the till to specify the amount being used to pay (choose from £10, £20, £50 or £100).
- Drag the appropriate amount of change from the till into the change area.
- Press the 'sale' button to check if the amount of change taken is correct.
- Press 'clear' to start a new sale.

What to do

This activity is designed to refine children's use of column subtraction. Ask the children to select an item and then drag it into the shopping basket. Press 'check-out' to move to the till on the next screen. After choosing the amount of cash to pay for the item, challenge the children to work out the change that should be given. Ask them to do this on their individual whiteboards and discuss the calculations in class. Finally, ask them to drag the notes and coins you would use for the change from the till into empty area on the left-hand side of the screen. Press 'sale' to check calculations. Press 'back to shop' to repeat the activity with another item.

Differentiation

Less confident: select items that will produce easier subtraction calculations in order to build confidence.
More confident: ask children to round the cost of each item and estimate the change before proceeding with the exact calculation.

Key questions

- *What change should be given?*
- *What coins could you use to give the change?*

'sale'
Press to check if amount paid is correct

'clear'
Press to start new sale

shopping items
Select and drag an item into the basket

'check-out'
Press to move to the till on the next screen

money
Drag exact money from till

Polygons (ITP)

Strand

Understanding shape

Learning objective

Identify, visualise and describe properties of rectangles, triangles and regular polygons

Type of starter

Refresh

Whiteboard tools

- Press the arrows on the square containing the number to specify the number of sides for your polygon.
- Press the square containing the number to show a regular polygon with the selected number of sides.
- Use the up and down arrows on the square containing the yellow triangle to increase or decrease the size of any polygon.
- Press the rotation sign to rotate the polygon.
- Press the ruler and protractor to measure the lengths of the sides and the size of the angles.

What to do

The aim of this activity is to identify the different regular polygons and investigate some of their properties. Invite children to come to the board to create any regular polygon with up to ten sides. Next, enlarge or rotate the polygon to see if it changes with either of these effects. Similarly, investigate the lengths of sides and angles of each polygon using the on-screen ruler and the protractor. Discuss with the children other properties – for example, which sides (if any) are parallel.

Differentiation

Less confident: ask children if they think the lengths of the sides appear to look equal in length as the regular polygon is enlarged. Check their predictions using the on-screen ruler.
More confident: ask children what happens to the size of the angles as the regular polygon is enlarged. Check their predictions by measuring the angles with the on-screen protractor.

Key questions

- *What is this shape called?*
- *What can you tell me about the lengths of the sides and the angles?*

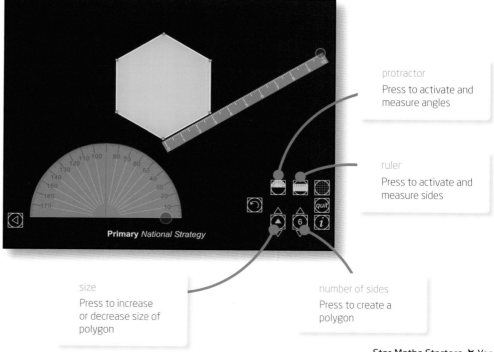

protractor
Press to activate and measure angles

ruler
Press to activate and measure sides

size
Press to increase or decrease size of polygon

number of sides
Press to create a polygon

Find the alien: coordinates

Strand

Understanding shape

Learning objective

Read and plot coordinates in the first quadrant

Type of starter

Reason

Whiteboard tools
● Type the x and y coordinates into the brackets to select a point on the grid.
● A keypad pops up automatically when you press on the brackets to enter a number.
● Press 'check' to confirm the choice.
● Press 'new' to start a new game with the alien in a different position.

What to do

The aim of the activity is to find a point on a 5 × 5 grid at which an alien is hiding. Tell the children that they should use coordinates to identify each point. The position of the alien is randomly selected each time. After each selection, a point will be revealed, some of which have other images such as a rocket or a planet hidden in them.

To narrow the selections down and prevent the activity becoming a guessing game, a message appears after each selection indicating how many points away from the alien (horizontally and/or vertically) the chosen coordinate is. Children should respond positively to this activity and will start to develop logical processes through the careful selection of points to find the alien in the fewest selections.

Differentiation

Less confident: ask children for coordinates early in the activity while the choice of a point is still quite random, to ensure that they understand the horizontal and vertical numbering system.
More confident: ask children about possible strategies to find the alien in the smallest number of goes.

Key questions

● *How can you describe, for example, the point in the top-left hand corner using x and y coordinates?*
● *Which possible point could the alien be in, now that we know the number of horizontal or vertical points from where he is hiding?*

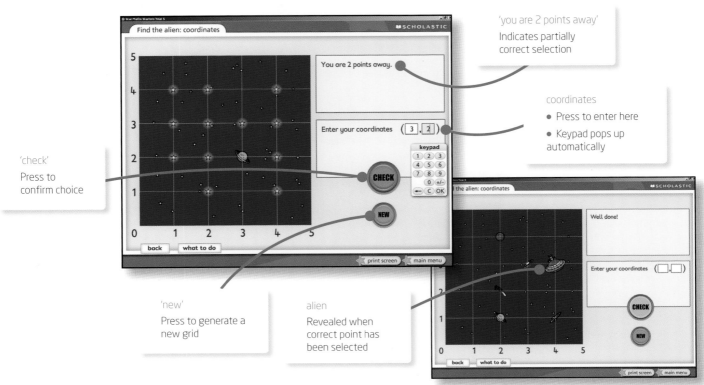

'check'
Press to confirm choice

'you are 2 points away'
Indicates partially correct selection

coordinates
● Press to enter here
● Keypad pops up automatically

'new'
Press to generate a new grid

alien
Revealed when correct point has been selected

Coordinates (ITP)

Strand

Understanding shape

Learning objective

Read and plot coordinates in the first quadrant

Type of starter

Refine

Whiteboard tools

- Press the 'new marker' button to add an unlabelled marker to the grid. Use the arrows on either side to position it.
- Move the cross-hair over any marker and press the 'coordinates' button to show or hide the coordinates.
- Although only one quadrant is used for this activity, up to four quadrants can be used if required.

What to do

The aim of this activity is to refine strategies used by the children when identifying coordinates. The activity automatically opens in a single quadrant. Create a series of markers by selecting a new marker and placing it on the grid. (If more than one marker is selected they will place themselves on top of each other until moved.) Ask the class to identify the coordinates marked using their individual whiteboards (briefly revise how to write coordinates). Next, activate the cross-hair and turn on the coordinates marker. The cross-hair can be manually placed anywhere on the grid and will automatically reveal its current coordinate. Check results.

Differentiation

Less confident: place a number of markers on either the vertical or horizontal axis so that when children are identifying the coordinate they can see the relationship between the x and y axis numbers.

More confident: introduce the children to working with two or four quadrants. Investigate how coordinates change across the four quadrants.

Key questions

- *Where else would we commonly find coordinates?* (Consider maps such as OS or a local A-Z, reference an online mapping site such as Multi-map or Google Maps, or games like battleships.)
- *What strategies or tips could we use to remember the order of numbers?*

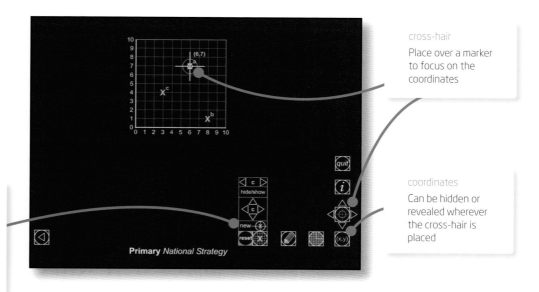

cross-hair
Place over a marker to focus on the coordinates

new marker
- Press to create new marker
- Can either be placed manually around the grid or moved using the arrows

coordinates
Can be hidden or revealed wherever the cross-hair is placed

Reflection square

Strand

Understanding shape

Learning objective

Complete patterns with up to two lines of symmetry; draw the position of a shape after a reflection

Type of starter

Refine

Whiteboard tools

- Use the 'options' menu to select the direction of the mirror line (horizontal, vertical or diagonal) and to specify the size of the grid.
- Press each square in the white area to draw a shape. When complete, press 'done'.
- Draw the reflection in the shaded area. When complete, press 'done'.
- Press on a white or coloured square if you wish to change either the object or the image.
- Press 'check' to see if the reflection drawn is correct.

What to do

Start by drawing a shape with two lines of symmetry. This activity offers a choice of reflection in the vertical axis, the horizontal axis, both vertical and horizontal axes, or a diagonal line. Draw a shape on the grid and challenge the children to draw its reflection. Once they are familiar with the aim of the starter, encourage them to come to the board to build an object with two lines of symmetry themselves and also, of course, to draw the reflected image.

Differentiation

Less confident: limit the activity to one line of symmetry initially.
More confident: select the option to draw the reflection of a complex shape in a diagonal line, or parallel to one edge, which will probably stretch even the most confident learners.

Key questions

- *How do you know that your pattern is symmetrical?*
- *Where would the reflection of this pattern be?*

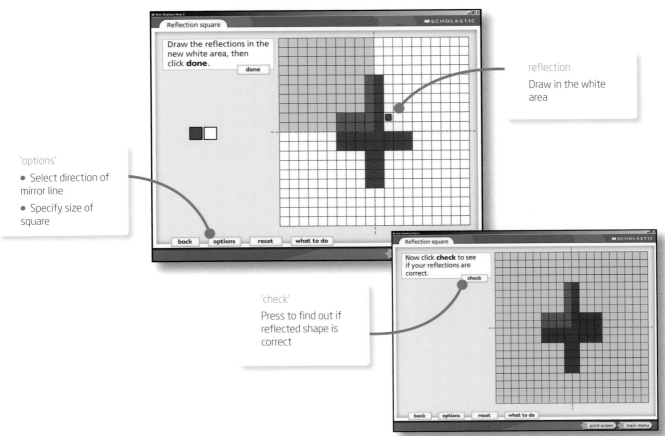

reflection
Draw in the white area

'options'
- Select direction of mirror line
- Specify size of square

'check'
Press to find out if reflected shape is correct

Maps and directions

Strand

Understanding shape

Learning objective

Estimate acute and obtuse angles to a suitable degree of accuracy

Type of starter

Reason

Whiteboard tools

- Press 'new' to generate a map with three objects to collect and some routes blocked.
- Drag and drop the directions and movements cards to prepare a suitable route for the lorry to follow. Select one direction card and one movement card each time.
- Press 'move' to confirm the selection. The recycling lorry will then move along the route and pause at the next point to wait for the next instruction.
- Press 'show route' to display the directions selected so far, and the trail.
- View the box at the top of the screen to identify which items the lorry has collected along the route.

What to do

This activity develops children's use of angles and turning. From a given starting point, ask the children for directions to guide the lorry to the recycling centre using the direction and movement cards on the screen as prompts. Drag and drop each card into place to build up the route. More than one route is available and some routes include barriers or objects to collect, so the quickest route is not necessarily the best. At any time during the activity, you can press the 'show route' button to check the lorry's progress. Encourage the children to check and challenge the route at this stage and start again if necessary. For each step, press 'move' to confirm the chosen instructions, and the lorry will move along the route accordingly. Once the lorry has collected all three recycling bins, select the appropriate instructions to move it to the recycling centre to deposit its contents. Make sure that at all times the children use the correct mathematical vocabulary when selecting an instruction from the screen.

Differentiation

Less confident: ask children questions that only require the use of 90° turns at first. Give them copies of the photocopiable 'Maps and directions' sheet on page 46 as additional support.

More confident: ask children for alternative ways of giving the same directions (for example, rotating through 135° from North is the same as moving SE).

Key questions

- *What is the most direct way to move from this point to that?*
- *Are there any alternative ways of moving from this point to that?*

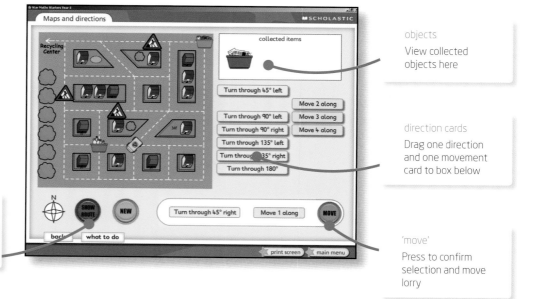

objects
View collected objects here

direction cards
Drag one direction and one movement card to box below

'show route'
Press to see directions selected so far and trail

'move'
Press to confirm selection and move lorry

Fixing points (ITP): measuring polygons

Strand

Understanding shape

Learning objective

Measure acute and obtuse angles using a protractor

Type of starter

Refresh

Whiteboard tools

- Specify the size of the grid through the 'grid size' menu.
- Press on any number of points on the grid to create a polygon.
- Use the protractor to measure the angles.
- Press the 'angles display' button to check answers.
- Press 'reset' to remove any lines drawn.

What to do

This activity provides a good demonstration of how to use a protractor. It enables polygons of different shapes and sizes to be drawn very quickly and accurately. Create a regular or irregular polygon by pressing on any number of points on the grid. These will automatically be lettered and will join up to form the required shape. Activate the protractor tool and use it to measure the different angles. Ask the children to read the angles and write them on their individual whiteboards. Press the 'angles display' button and select the relevant question mark to check whether they are correct.

Differentiation

Less confident: provide support in using a protractor by asking children to come to the board and use the on-screen protractor to measure the angles themselves.
More confident: ask children to measure the angles of different triangles and then add the three angles together. Question them about their results.

Key questions

- *At what point should the protractor be positioned to measure an angle?*
- *Which of these angles are acute and which are obtuse? Why?*

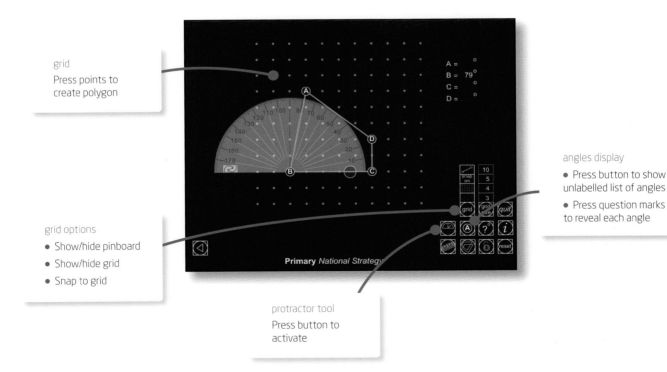

grid
Press points to create polygon

grid options
- Show/hide pinboard
- Show/hide grid
- Snap to grid

protractor tool
Press button to activate

angles display
- Press button to show unlabelled list of angles
- Press question marks to reveal each angle

Weighing scales

Strand

Measuring

Learning objective

Convert larger to smaller units using decimals to one place (eg change 2.6kg to 2600g).

Type of starter

Read

Whiteboard tools
- Drag and drop items on the left of the screen into the pan or add some preset weights.
- On the analogue scale, turn the digital readout off or on, as required.
- Select 'options' to make changes to the divisions on the face of the scales.

What to do
The aim of this activity is to accurately read and convert kilos to grams or vice versa. Ask the children to write the weight (using decimal notation) on their individual whiteboards using the opposite notation on the screen (grams if kilograms are shown) and to show their partners. Assess any misconceptions or errors and ask children to explain how the face of the scales can help when reading the weight.

Repeat the activity over a number of sessions to check how quickly and confidently the children can read and convert the measurements on the scales.

Differentiation
Less confident: press the 'options' menu to increase the subdivisions on the face of the scales to 10.
More confident: ask: *What is the minimum number of weights that can be used to balance the food?* Record the initial weight of the food, then remove two items and record the new weight. Ask: *What is the difference between the two weights in grams and kilograms?*

Key questions
- *What is the weight of the different objects in grams and kilograms?*
- *What is the total weight of these two items in grams and kilograms?*

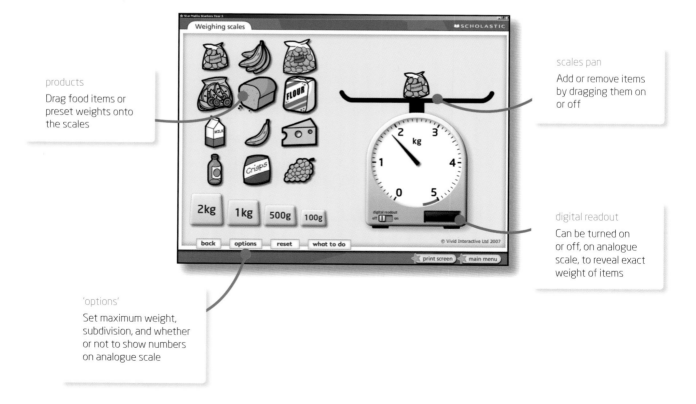

products
Drag food items or preset weights onto the scales

scales pan
Add or remove items by dragging them on or off

digital readout
Can be turned on or off, on analogue scale, to reveal exact weight of items

'options'
Set maximum weight, subdivision, and whether or not to show numbers on analogue scale

Thermometer (ITP)

Strand

Measuring

Learning objective

Interpret a reading that lies between two unnumbered divisions on a scale

Type of starter

Read

Whiteboard tools

- Use the maximum, minimum and interval buttons to adjust the thermometer settings as required.
- Drag the slider into position to select a current level.
- Previous level marker remains in place to allow calculation of difference.
- Fix or unfix previous level marker. When unfixed it will automatically move each time the slider is moved to give a new difference.
- Press buttons to show or hide the current temperature level, the difference between the previous and current levels, and the change that has taken place.

What to do

The aim of this activity is to be able to accurately read temperature at speed and to identify the change between the slider and previous level marker. Check that the children are confident in reading positive and negative temperature by changing the value with the slider. Once done, explain that the previous level indicator (the yellow arrow) shows what the temperature was previously and that we can change the temperature. The example below shows that the temperature has changed by -15°C and that the new temperature is 10°C. Each time the user changes the temperature with the slider, the yellow arrow will automatically change to give a new difference between the two (unless the 'lock' button has been selected, at which point the arrow will change to blue).

Differentiation

Less confident: the slider tool can be used to support accurate reading of the thermometer.
More confident: increase the scale. Discuss where very low/high temperatures might occur. Ask: *Have you experienced temperatures like this? If so, where?*

Key questions

- *How do the divisions help the user to read the thermometer?*
- *What strategies are you using when working out the difference, particularly if it is a negative change?*

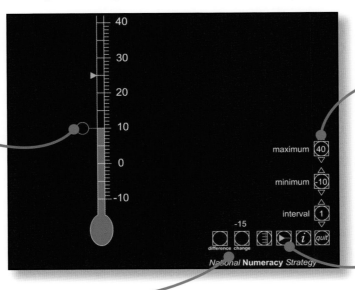

slider
- Move to any measurement
- When unlocked, the previous level marker (yellow arrow) will also change

maximum, minimum, interval buttons
Change preset amounts as required

fix/unfix previous level marker
- Locks marker to one place (coloured blue)
- When unlocked (yellow), arrow button will change with every change of slider to give new difference

value, difference and change indicators
When selected, these indicators show the change factors

Measuring jug

Strand

Measuring

Learning objective

Interpret a reading that lies between two unnumbered divisions on a scale

Type of starter

Refine

Whiteboard tools

● Press the 'options' button to set the following: set 'scale' to 100ml; set 'mode' to max only; set 'subdivisions' to none (to give 10ml intervals on the jug); set 'fill steps' to manual.
● Press 'in' to fill the jug, and press it again to stop filling.
● Press 'out' to empty the jug, and press it again to stop emptying.
● Press 'reset' to start again.

What to do

Tell the children that the jug can hold up to 100ml. Ask them how many millilitres they think each subdivision represents. Next, question individual children about the unmarked divisions and ask them to read these aloud. Fill the jug part way up to a certain level (for example, approximately 45ml) and then question them about the reading. Fill and empty the jug to find the difference between the two levels. Set some problems (see 'Key questions' below) and ask the children to write the answers on their individual whiteboards. Check the answers using the measuring jug. This activity may be extended by suggesting to the children that the jug holds 1000ml or 500ml rather than 100ml (press 'options' to amend the measurements appropriately).

Differentiation

Less confident: in the early stages, ask children to read the scale to the nearest 50ml mark.
More confident: challenge the children by asking if they can suggest a more accurate reading.

Key questions

● *A bottle of medicine holds 100ml. How many 5ml spoonfuls can be taken from the bottle?*
● *A bottle of chilli sauce holds 100ml. If a recipe requires one 15ml spoonful, how many times can the dish be made and how much is left over?*

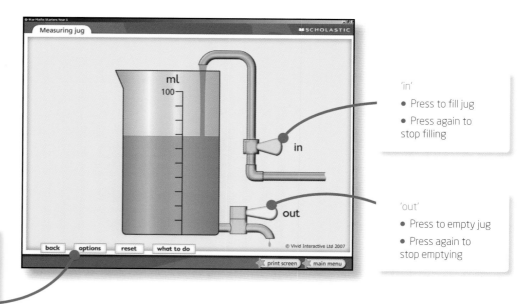

'options'
Select the following:
● scale: 100ml
● mode: max only
● subdivisions: none
● fill steps: manual

'in'
● Press to fill jug
● Press again to stop filling

'out'
● Press to empty jug
● Press again to stop emptying

Ruler (ITP)

Strand

Measuring

Learning objective

Draw and measure lines
to the nearest millimetre

Type of starter

Refine

Whiteboard tools

- Select the pencil from the drawing tools to draw lines. Press on the start and the end of the line you wish to draw, within the drawing area.
- Select wooden (opaque) or plastic (transparent) ruler style from the ruler menu.
- Use the ruler to measure lines by dragging it across the screen. Rotate the ruler by pressing and dragging the small circle at its far right end.
- Press the eraser button in the drawing tools menu to erase all lines and shapes drawn.

What to do

The aim of this starter is to refine the skills needed to draw and measure lines accurately. The activity opens with a blank square on the left-hand side. All lines/ shapes can only be drawn in that space. Start by drawing some lines on the board by dragging the pencil across the drawing space. Explain that the children are going to test their skill in reading centimetres and millimetres accurately and then later to draw accurately. Encourage them to estimate the size of the lines you have drawn, to the nearest millimetre, before using the on-screen ruler to measure them – explain that this needs to be done carefully so that an accurate measurement can be taken. Draw and measure up to five different lines before pressing the eraser button in the drawing tools menu to clear the board.

Explain that the children are now going to accurately draw lines that are up to 10cm in length on their whiteboards and on the interactive whiteboard. Start by asking the class to draw a 5cm and 8cm line to assess their accuracy. Encourage the children to support one another. Then ask for some suggested challenging measurements, such as 5.4cm. Assess accuracy in measurement and drawing.

Differentiation

Less confident: encourage these learners to estimate line lengths by using a known line marker (for example, a line that measures 5cm) as a guide.
More confident: draw a polygon on the board and measure some of its sides. Challenge the children to accurately estimate and then measure the remaining sides.

Key questions

- *Can you estimate how long you think the line is?*
- *How would we be able to measure lines that are longer than the ruler?*

ruler
- Drag to measure lines
- Press and drag circle on far right to rotate

pencil

Drag across drawing area, pressing on start and end points to draw line

drawing tools menu
Select required option:
- Draw line
- Draw solid shape
- Erase all lines and shapes

ruler menu
- Select wooden (opaque) or plastic (transparent) ruler
- Choose to show or hide ruler scale

Primary *National Strategy*

Area (ITP)

Strand

Measuring

Learning objective

Measure and calculate the perimeter of regular and irregular polygons

Type of starter

Rehearse

Whiteboard tools

- Specify the size of grid required through the 'grid size' menu.
- Press the 'pinboard' button to change the grid to a pinboard, if required.
- Press the 'shape colour' button to select from a range of colours for solid shapes.
- Use the 'shape controls' menu to automatically add your selected solid shape to one square space on the grid.
- Press the 'reset' button to clear solid shapes from the grid.
- Use the 'elastic band' tool to access a virtual elastic band that can be stretched around the corners of the grid.

What to do

The aim of this starter is to rehearse the skills and strategies needed to find the perimeter of a polygon. Below are examples of how polygons can be created by using either the automatic shape fill or elastic band buttons. Once a shape is created, review how to find its perimeter and what strategies the children might use. The level of complexity and challenge can be altered, particularly when using the elastic band tool, to quickly develop and test individual or group theories.

Differentiation

Less confident: use the automatic shape button to create regular polygon shapes. Add one triangle at a time to demonstrate how the perimeter increases.
More confident: use the elastic band tool to create more challenging polygons.

Key questions

- *If we didn't have a ruler, how could we estimate the size of this shape?*
- *Does it make any difference if the shape is made out of an elastic band or solid blocks?*

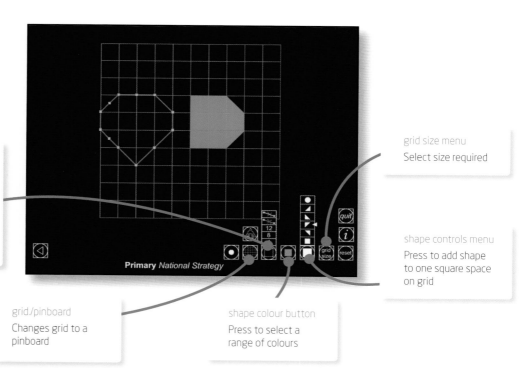

elastic band menu
- Select number of points for elastic band
- Select up to two elastic bands at a time
- Press buttons to erase shapes drawn

grid size menu
Select size required

shape controls menu
Press to add shape to one square space on grid

grid./pinboard
Changes grid to a pinboard

shape colour button
Press to select a range of colours

Clocks: time difference using 24-hour time

Strand

Measuring

Learning objective

Read time using 24-hour clock notation

Type of starter

Read

Whiteboard tools

● Press the 'randomise' button to select a random digital or analogue time on the clocks.
● Drag the clock hands manually to move the time on the analogue clock; set the hour and minutes on the digital clock by pressing the + and − signs.
● 'options' button: use this to specify the settings for the 'randomise' functions. You can also choose to link the hour and minutes hands on the analogue clock.

What to do

The aim of this activity is to work out, in hours and minutes, the difference between the two clocks. Start by pressing the 'randomise' button under the analogue clock and ask the class to call out the time. Repeat three or four times to assess that the children are able to read the time to the nearest minute with confidence. Next, press the 'randomise' button on both the analogue and digital clocks and ask the children to work out the time difference between the two. The digital clock will automatically show 24-hour time so it would be useful to assess that all the children can translate 24-hour time into am and pm.

Differentiation

Less confident: assess that the group can read 24-hour time accurately. Randomly select a time that is beyond 12 midday to demonstrate 24-hour time and ask one of the children to show the time on the analogue clock by dragging the hands.
More confident: introduce the concept of world time. Point out that Chicago, for example, is six hours behind GMT time and that Paris is one hour ahead. Ask: *When it is 6.30 here, what time would it be in Chicago and Paris?*

Key questions

● *How can we make rough estimates between the times?*
● *What is the difference between am and pm (am = antemeridian, pm = post meridian) and why does it matter?*

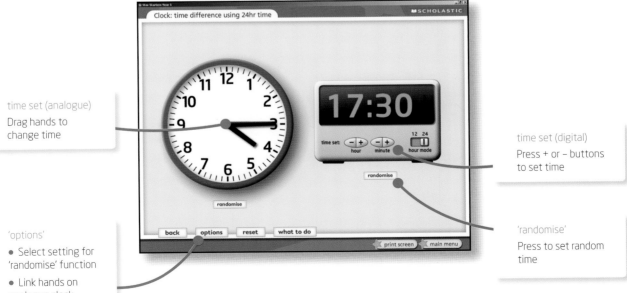

time set (analogue)
Drag hands to change time

time set (digital)
Press + or − buttons to set time

'options'
● Select setting for 'randomise' function
● Link hands on analogue clock

'randomise'
Press to set random time

Data handling (ITP)

Strand

Handling data

Learning objective

Answer a set of questions by collecting, selecting and organising relevant data; use ICT to present features

Type of starter

Read

Whiteboard tools
- Press the 'data' button to either reveal preset data or the option to enter your own data.
- Press the bar chart icon to create a bar chart from the data table.
- Choose to show or hide elements of the data table including the colour key, titles, numbers and percentages.
- Use the 'increase/decrease' buttons to manually change the data.
- Press the 'max' button and type in the maximum value on the numerical axis when creating your own data. The input number range is 0.9 to 90000.

What to do

The aim of this starter is to present preset data to the children in order that they can analyse and interpret its information. The activity launches as a blank page; as a suggestion it is useful to start with the preset data on 'Our favourite drinks'. With this activity it may be useful to present two on the screen at once so that they can be compared. It is worth analysing the categories and data for each drink - identify other flavours and types of drink (for example, juices are not shown). Does this reflect the class's tastes? Using the increase/decrease buttons, adapt the bar chart so that it shows the class results. Can any comparisons with the other data be made? What are the differences, and why do we think that is so? (For example, population changes, urban or rural differences, and so on.)

Differentiation

Less confident: encourage these learners to read the bars using only the scale (hide the numbers and reveal at the end).
More confident: review the data as a pie chart. Shown in this way, what general statements can be made about the data? Could the data be translated into fractions?

Key questions
- *What statements about the data can you make before reading any figures?*
- *Can you identify any equivalent fractions?*

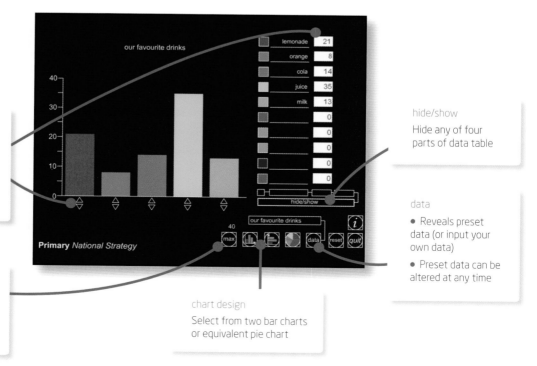

increase /decrease
Use either arrows under each bar to change total or highlight number in data table and overtype

max
Press when creating your own data and type maximum value for numerical axis

chart design
Select from two bar charts or equivalent pie chart

hide/show
Hide any of four parts of data table

data
- Reveals preset data (or input your own data)
- Preset data can be altered at any time

Targets

- Find the target numbers using the cards below.

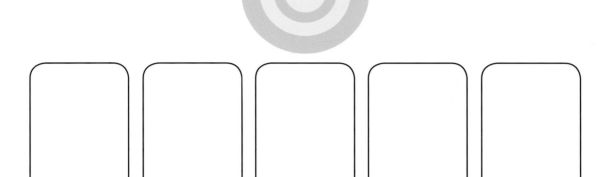

- How I worked out the target answer.

_____

_____

_____

_____

_____

_____

_____

_____

Name _____   Date _____

Fairground: counting below zero

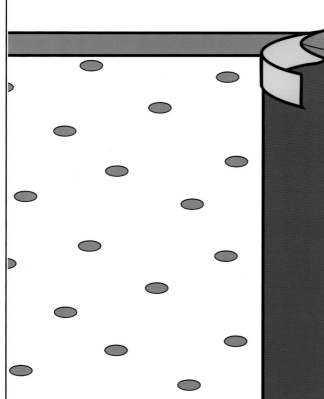
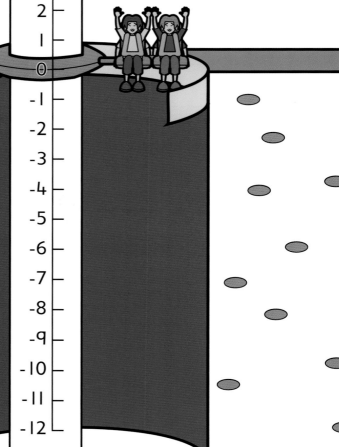

Star Maths Starters ★ Year 5
PHOTOCOPIABLE

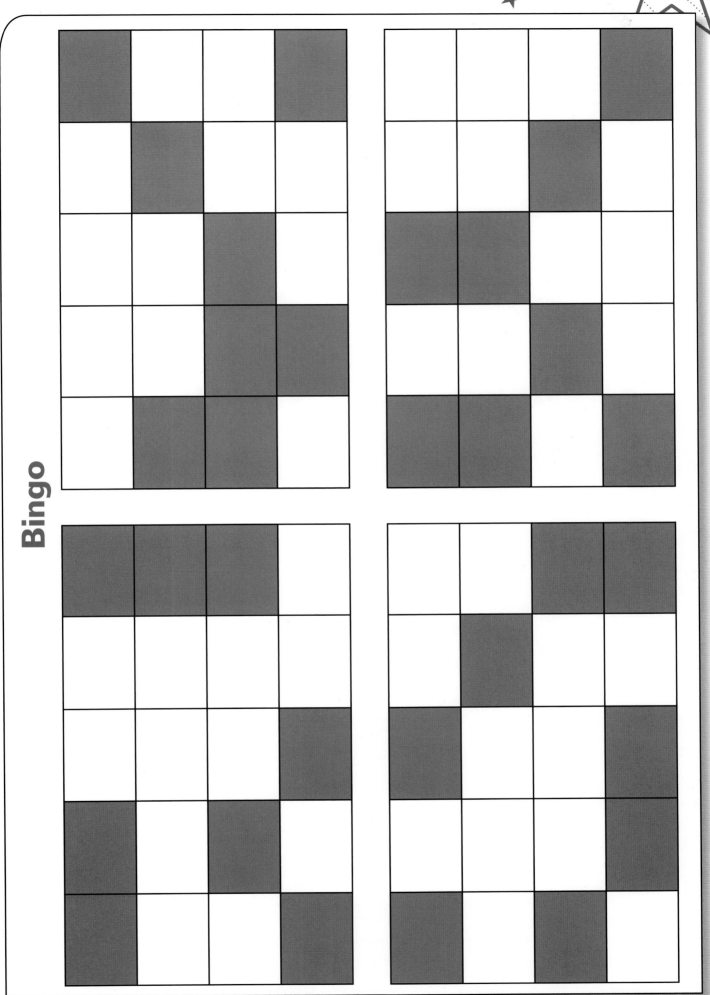

Maps and directions

◾ Plan your route using the map below.

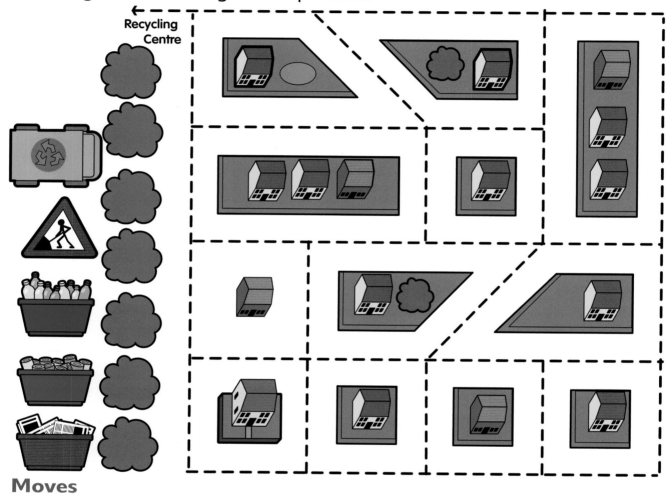

Recycling Centre

Moves

_____

_____

_____

_____

_____

_____

_____

_____

Star Maths Starters diary page

Name of Star Starter	PNS objectives covered	How was activity used	Date activity was used

Also available in this series:

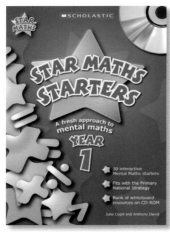

ISBN 978-1407-10007-4

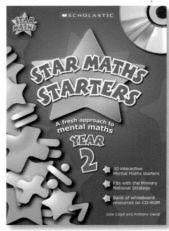

ISBN 978-1407-10008-1

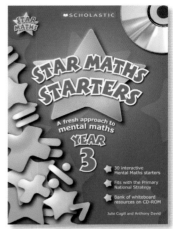

ISBN 978-1407-10009-8

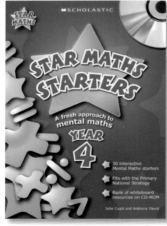

ISBN 978-1407-10010-4

ISBN 978-1407-10011-1

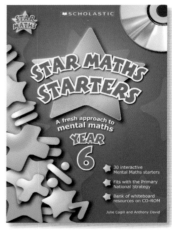

ISBN 978-1407-10012-8

ISBN 978-1407-10031-9

ISBN 978-1407-10032-6

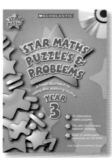

ISBN 978-1407-10033-3

ISBN 978-1407-10034-0

ISBN 978-1407-10035-7

ISBN 978-1407-10036-4

To find out more, call: 0845 603 9091
or visit our website www.scholastic.co.uk